How to
Destroy a Monster That Feeds on Itself

NORMAN POWELL

WestBow
PRESS
A DIVISION OF THOMAS NELSON

WestBow Press books may be ordered through booksellers or by contacting:

WestBow Press
A Division of Thomas Nelson
1663 Liberty Drive
Bloomington, IN 47403
www.westbowpress.com
1-(866) 928-1240

ISBN: 978-1-4908-0055-4 (sc)

Library of Congress Control Number: 2013912076

Printed in the United States of America.

WestBow Press rev. date: 7/8/2013

*In memory of my dear departed mother
who taught me so much and laid the
foundation for me to seek the truth.*

ACKNOWLEDGEMENTS

My sincere thanks go to Win Thompkins and the members of our spiritual study group, including Dale, Kelvin, Lil' Kevin and Valerie Thompkins who have so graciously provided accommodations and other amenities for our life study group year in and year out.

Special thanks to a very dear friend Joanne Muire for encouraging me to write this book and to Theresa Seldon for igniting the fire which led to publishing the book.

Dr. Wayne W. Dyer for his insight as written in his book "Your Sacred Self: Making the decision to be free."

PREFACE

I was inspired to write this book when I tapped into the divine spirit within me. I was born on Friday, October 13th, and I was marked by carnal thinking to be an unlucky individual all my life. However, my mother was tuned in to the spirit of her true self and she was able to provide for my six siblings and me abundantly in spite of the absence of our father, the absence of a formal education, and most importantly the absence of carnal minded thinking…she never acquired a driving license or owned an automobile.

Although we were considered poor (by carnal standards), we always had more than enough of what we needed. My mother would always have an abundance of life supporting and nourishing sources. It was back in the day when the art of *"canning"* was prevalent. Canning was the preservation of meats, vegetables, or other foods by sealing them in an airtight can or jar. We always had food stored up for consumption in the future. I remember when anyone came by our house, whether it was the weekly visit by the insurance man, the Sunday visit by the pastor and congregation members or just the neighbors dropping by, my mother would not let them leave without giving them something…anything.

We grew up in a small town on a six acre parcel of land. Amazingly my mother was able to utilize every inch of this property to plant seeds that would produce fruits, vegetables, and about any other thing you could name. We enjoyed fresh healthy harvests from the garden each day. We would travel to the nearest town once a month for items we could not grow on the land.

I was the youngest of seven children and believe me, within myself, I created a monster that would eventually feed on itself. I discovered early on that as the youngest child I had special favor with my mother. I became very manipulative and I knew exactly what role to play when it came to having my own way.

What I didn't realize was that these roles would dictate how I would live my life in the future. I became absorbed with myself and was guided by this absorption to never be totally satisfied with anything I was involved in. Little did I know, I was allowing a false image of myself to set the stage for my personal journey through life.

Throughout my life, I felt that something was missing. I was constantly seeking something but not sure exactly what it was. I was told to get a good education...I did. I was told to get a good job...I did. I was told to get married and start a family...I did. I was told to stay out of trouble...I did. I was told to go to church...I did. I was told to start my own business...I did. All of these things I did, but I still felt something was missing. My false self was urging me to overachieve and show the world I could be successful. Indeed, I succeeded at a lot of things, but the inner peace I desired was still missing. I can remember contributing to a building fund each Sunday in church and to this day, I have not seen a building. I was told that all

I had to do was give 10% of my earnings to the church and I would reap the benefit of a hundred fold return. Instead of a return, things only got worse. And there were certain members of the congregation that would say the same prayer and repeat the same testimony every Sunday. Obviously their prayers weren't being answered. If they were, there would be no reason to keep praying for the same thing. I would run into some of them out partying on the Saturday night before, and they would give me that look as if I had better not say anything.

I found that attending church was not the answer... Something was still missing. Although we were raised in the church, my mother was not a "church going" person. Through tradition, she would send us off with other members of the family as she stayed home and read the Bible. From time to time my mother would read scriptures from the Bible aloud to make a point; however I didn't understand what point she was trying to make. Now I know why I didn't understand and now I know why those individuals continued to repeat the same prayers every Sunday. What was missing in my life and theirs was a higher level of understanding. After joining a small

Bible study group, my way of thinking changed. The fact is, I was allowing carnality -the Ego- to dictate and control my life's decisions. ***Carnal minded people cannot communicate with the true divine spirit in themselves. Those people were praying in vain.*** Needless to say, I started to program myself to destroy the monster that I had allowed to infiltrate my mind and feed on itself. I was encouraged by friends and family members to go to church more, and that I would find the answer there. Quite the contrary, once I started attending church on a regular basis I was more confused than ever. To be true to yourself and reach a higher level of understanding, you <u>MUST</u> tap into the spirit of Christ that dwells within you and allow it to guide you through life…not the church, not the pastor, not your family, not your friends, not your neighbors, not your co-workers, not your acquaintances…not anything outside of you. ***That was my mother's secret!*** The light that dwelled in my mother was so great that it illuminated areas around her. Thus, my siblings and I were exposed to the light and were able to see and maneuver around or avoid the dark areas in our lives.

For a woman who had less than a 4th grade education, she had an enormous amount of wisdom. I knew that she was special and I knew that she was driven by something from within, but I didn't know what it was. She possessed a mystical power that allowed her to plant any kind of seed and reap a beautiful harvest that garnered her nickname "*lady with the green thumb.*" It wasn't until I became a man and was able to tap into my true self that I realized what she possessed. Against insurmountable odds (according to the carnal mind), my mother was able to provide not only for my six siblings and me, but also for an entire community. *It was indeed the spirit of Christ that dictated her every move in life.* She was a wonderful woman and I miss her.

Because of the nature of this subject, I don't expect that everyone will agree with me on my assessment as recorded in this book. However, it is based on my personal awakening and personal experiences that are evidence of justification and truth for this writing.

CONTENTS

PART ONE

ACKNOWLEDGEMENT OF THE MONSTER

We've all been taught to look outside ourselves for sustenance—to look beyond the self for power, love, prosperity, health, happiness and spiritual fulfillment. We've been conditioned to believe we get life's bounty from somewhere outside ourselves. But it's possible to reverse our gaze from outward to inward. And when we do, we find an energy we've sensed but not previously identified.

—Dr. Wayne W. Dyer

This book is written to expose the monster that dwells in us called "carnality." Some refer to carnality as the "Ego," an exaggerated sense of self that is most in touch with external reality and focuses on the desires of the flesh; so much so, that it will destroy every part of your being by convincing you that it is you. It is a "mind set" that will take every opportunity to create confusion and wreak havoc on your life. It is the exact opposite of the true life giving principle within a living being called "spirit."

THE DEFINITION OF "EGO"

Ego-The American Heritage Dictionary defines Ego as the personality component of *self* that most immediately controls behavior and is in touch mostly with "*external reality.*"

It will consistently try to divert you away from your true self, which is the embodiment of the spirit of Christ. It will feed on itself and bloat itself with deceit, Jealousy, illusion, fear, division and other methods of trickery that will lead you down a path of total destruction. *The Ego is so powerful that many humans never even get a glimpse of their true divine self throughout their entire life.* It will continuously stack false images on top of each other until your true divine self is buried so deep within you that you never come in contact with it.

The Ego is a master of disguise and can appear at anytime and anyplace at its own discretion. It will put you in a box and tell you that you are limited to experience only certain parts of life that it feels you should experience. It goes to extreme lengths to conceal the truth…that you are not limited and that you are a being of divine energy. When tapped into, this energy can perform miracles and create experiences of inner bliss which projects outward qualities such as love, understanding, kindness, joyfulness and a feeling of oneness. ***OH, WHAT A WONDERFUL WORLD IT COULD BE!***

From the moment of conception, your Ego starts to take root and begins to download its deception in your mind through an environment it has perpetuated from generation to generation. It will have you looking outside yourself for life's fulfillment. It will inform you that the physical world is all you need while not revealing to you that the physical world has limitations. It will convince you to manage the way you appear to others and to seek help from some external source for survival. Its mission is to keep you from making contact with the real you (one of divination) because it knows that if you connect with the real you, there are no limitations and being the coward it is, the Ego must flee.

You see, once you discover the nature of your true divine self, you will begin to regulate the Ego and you will realize that you have a purpose for being here and that purpose will not be found in the physical world. As an analogy, let's just say that your mind is the equivalent of an automobile; and it has two passengers, the Ego and your true divine self (the spirit of Christ). If the Ego is the driver, you will never reach your destination. It will keep you looping "around and around" in circles with no purpose. Once you realize this through the awareness of your true divine self, you will remove the Ego from the driver's seat and tell it to take a seat in the back of the car. Once your true divine self starts to drive, you will be on your way to a life of total bliss. Not only will you be able to see your destination in the distance, but you will also be guided on a remarkable journey towards it.

The Ego is a master designer of masks. In the scenario where the Ego is driving the car, you can count on it having a trunk full of masks. Once you tap into your true divine self, you will not only be able to recognize the masks the Ego created for you, but you will also be able to recognize the masks of others that are allowing the Ego to drive their automobile. The Ego uses masks to try to conceal itself and gain notoriety as the driving force within you. It will prey on the minds of the weak, those that have not become aware of their true divine self.

Since the Ego is rooted from conception and perpetuated by outside forces continuously, it maintains a stronghold on the mind that is not easy to destroy. It constantly feeds on itself and after a while, it becomes self-sustaining. It will have you striving to get "things" as confirmation that you are successful in this life. It creates a mindset of the greatest illusive nature that will have you burdened down with debt to get these things. Its victory comes when you are a slave to earthly things which really have no value at all in the spirit realm.

The Ego thrives on "mind control," causing you to make decisions that will inevitably hurt you. The most ironic part of it all is that the Ego will then have you looking to it for a solution to these very same hurts caused by those decisions. In this case, the Ego will respond by influencing you to make more decisions that will continue to hurt you. These decisions are carefully calculated by the Ego to lead you further and further away from ever coming in contact with your true divine self.

All of these false self traits produced by the Ego are grounded in "fear." Sometimes these fears are so masterfully disguised that we don't recognize them and allow them to control our lives. We spend a lifetime listening to the Ego as it guides us in circles with no intent of ever allowing us to realize the full potential of our true divine selves.

From a biblical perspective, you can find reference to the carnal mind in ROMANS, Chapter 8 verses 5-8 (King James Version of the Bible).

NEW TESTAMENT (ROMANS 8:5-8)

5   For they that are after the flesh do mind the things of the flesh; but they that are after the spirit the things of the spirit.

6 For to be carnally minded is death; but to be spiritually minded is life and peace.

7 Because the carnal mind is enmity against God: for it is not subject to the law of God, neither indeed can it be.

8 So then they that are in the flesh cannot please God.

If you were able to put the Ego under a microscope, you would see something that might look like a bee hive…a frenzy of thought patterns that are constantly reinforcing the belief that the Ego is you. So much so that you will even argue that it is you. However, in reality these thoughts induced by the Ego are grounded in fear and doubt and are perpetuated from generation to generation. In other words, you inherited these thoughts from others.

When embedded in you, these thoughts initiate actions that produce other similar thoughts of the same kind and pretty soon your garden or vineyard (mind) produces a harvest full of these self-doubting thoughts that in turn produce more self-doubting thoughts and so on…

Understand that there will always be conflict. There will be individuals around you that are very protective of the Ego and they will want to dictate to you how they want you to behave. Example: someone tells you that a person is inferior to you and you should not associate with that person. Well, I got news for you. God has no respect of person and if you think this way, you have not tapped into the God within you. In addition, there will be those who believe it is blasphemous to speak of God being within us.

Dr. Wayne Dyer touches on the Ego in this telling passage: *The Ego is your false self. Your true self is eternal. It is the God force within you that provides the energy for you to roam around in the clothes you call your body—a quiet, empty space surrounded by form. Believing you are only the physical self, the body enclosing the energy, is a false belief.*

However, there is hope…you can destroy this monster. So what does it take to destroy this monster called the Ego and pursue the true divine self?

PART TWO

IDENTIFYING WHAT THIS MONSTER FEEDS ON

First, we must identify what the Ego feeds on, and then we can **put it on a diet**. This process will not occur overnight; however, by getting in touch with your true divine self and "staying awake" to your true divine self, your thinking will be linked to the spirit realm which will destroy this monster called the Ego. The Ego feeds on false perception of self through mind messages that focus on self. The following self concepts feed the Ego.

THE EGO (CARNAL)
DEFINITION OF "SELF"

Self-The Ego's definition of self is an individual concerned with one's own interests, welfare, or advantage. It focuses on me, myself, yourself, himself, or herself. This definition alone permeates individuality and moves one away from the spiritual concept of "oneness".

The Ego operates in darkness and plants seeds of certain elements of "Self" that will lead to a "Monster" that feeds on itself. It will have you stumbling all over yourself and, just as walking in darkness, you won't be able to see it coming. The following are some of these elements:

Self-**abasement**-Degrading, disgraceful...we witness displays of self-abasement daily in our lives. It is so commonly used by the Ego that we simply accept it as a way of life.

Self-**absorption**-Absorbed in oneself, full of oneself...the Ego likes this one; it will have you believing you are better than everyone else.

Self-**aggrandizement**-The practice of making oneself greater, more important than others... the Ego realizes that it does not have a chance once you find your true self so it lures you into thinking that you are something you are not.

Self-**Centered**-Selfish, egocentric...the Ego likes attention so it creates thought patterns within you that focus only on self.

Self-**Conceit**-A high opinion of oneself, vanity... the Ego utilizes self-conceit to influence you to boast excessively about your appearance, your possessions and your accomplishments.

Self-**condemnation**-Expressing disapproval of oneself...the Ego is worthless and until you discover the true you, it will have you thinking you are worthless.

Self-**consciousness**-Uncomfortably conscious of one's appearance or manner; ill at ease...the Ego uses this to produce masks for every occasion. It will dictate to you that you have to put on a certain mask to fit in different situations. It will have you riding around with a trunk full of masks.

***Self*-deception**-The act of deceiving oneself or the state of being deceived by oneself...this is the platform from which the Ego works. Its primary goal is to deceive you into believing that it is you.

***Self*-defeating**-Injurious to one's or its own purposes and welfare...the Ego strives to deter you away from your true purpose in life "by any means necessary."

***Self*-delusion**-A false belief, an illusion...in its box, the Ego has an arsenal of tricks and gadgets to create illusions that appear to be unequivocally real.

***Self*-doubt**-Lack of confidence in oneself...the Ego will lead you to believe you have no power within yourself and that your life is driven by outside forces.

***Self*-exaltation**-To glorify, praise oneself...the Ego uses this to deceive you that your life is controlled by it and not by the divine spirit that lives in you.

Self-**importance**-An excessively high opinion of one's own importance...feeding on this concept, the Ego will have you in what is termed a "want to be" state.

Self-**imposed**-Victimized by oneself...in this case the "oneself" is the Ego. It will make you a victim of its own doing and have you believing it is actually you that is the perpetrator.

Self-**induced**-Induced by oneself...the Ego leads by persuasion. It has the ability to present false incentives to move you to actions that will lead directly to destruction.

Self-**indulgence**-Excessive indulgence of one's own appetites and desires...the Ego has an insatiable appetite for "things" and "wants" and "desires." It creates a hole in your life that can never be filled.

Self-**interest**-Selfish regard for one's personal advantage or interest; gain...the Ego will constantly influence your thoughts to focus on illusions designed specifically for you to consider your personal gain in all that you do.

Selfish-Concerned only with oneself…this is a highly visible trait of the Ego. It does not care about what the real you wants, it wants everything for itself.

Self-pity-Excessive pity for oneself…the Ego will have you thinking all is loss and you are nothing. It will have you basking in darkness and looking for viable solutions in places where solutions don't exist.

Self-reproach-The act of blaming oneself for a fault or mistake…the Ego is quick to have you blaming yourself for mistakes or faults that it enacted in your life, not you.

Self-righteousness-Smugly sure of one's righteousness…the Ego will send you off on a wild goose chase filled with illusions of righteousness. Many people are so caught up in religion that they are driven further and further away from the truth, with the Ego convincing them that they are right.

Self-serving-Furthering one's own interest…the Ego will have you constantly calculating at any cost how you will obtain an upper hand in any and all situations.

Man subconsciously recognizes these self traits of the Ego as he refers to others as having an "*ego problem*" or to one as "*ego tripping*". The natural law states that when a seed is planted, it can only produce one of its own kind. If you plant a watermelon seed, you are going to get a watermelon, not a cantaloupe.

The same is with the Ego planting these self serving traits; you are only going to get a self serving product.

The planting of these seeds provide you with an idea…and an idea only…of who you are. It is non-existent, it is an illusion and it can only plant illusions. It paints external pictures, produces external music, and writes external books…all so that you will focus on the outside for determining your inside. Probably the most misguiding force used by the Ego is the prospect of religion and the concept of attending church as a complete method for achieving favor and salvation for your soul.

Being considered religious and spiritual are two different things. I have been around a number of people that consider themselves religious. While interacting with them, I am left with the feeling that they are imprisoned in dungeons of frustration. When asked "how are you?" Some respond "*blessed and highly favored.*" Then, when you ask "how is that?" in essence, they respond …I have a nice house, I have a nice car, I'm able to pay my bills and give my tithe to the church, or I have lots of food at the house to eat.

When they continue to communicate, being in a state of unawareness, they inevitably start complaining about the jobs they have to do to keep these things, the problems they are having with their children, the sicknesses they are dealing with, and the hope that one day they will be able to retire from all this. ***These are all dungeons that have been created by the Ego.***

In the spiritual realm, the realm of the true divine self, these things become "*meaningless chatter*"… they do not exist. No longer will you need to accumulate things and seek confirmation from others. You will experience a connectedness with the true source of all your needs that the Ego's illusions couldn't even begin to comprehend.

PART THREE

PUTTING THIS MONSTER ON A DIET

Once we recognize the self concepts the Ego feeds on, we can implement a plan to put it on a diet. The first thing is to acknowledge that the Ego is a driving force in your life. Until you do this, the monster will not only continue to abide in you, but it will also continue to guide you toward self-destruction.

Most people are misguided...many of them through false prophets and organized religion... to believe that their help cometh from a source outside of themselves. I witness daily individuals that profess to be "holier than thou." They think that they have to go to church to seek salvation and truth.

Basically we have to rid ourselves of egotistical thoughts, regardless of what others may think. You must realize that you have the gift of the spirit of Christ in you. It is a *gift*...you can't work for it, you can't buy it, you can't barter for it, you can't steal it, you can't get it by attending church, you can't get it through material possessions, and you can't get it through any worldly activity.

It is *free* and all you have to do is look inside yourself, **confess that it is in you and let it guide you**. Once you do this, you will awaken to a whole new experience of life where challenges do not exist, only opportunities.

From a biblical perspective, you can find reference to spiritual gifts in King James Version of the Bible:

NEW TESTAMENT (ST. JOHN 14:17)

17 Even the spirit of truth; whom the world cannot receive, because it seeth him not,

neither knoweth him: but ye know him; for he dwelleth with you, and shall be in you.

NEW TESTAMENT (ROMANS 8:9-13)

9 But ye are not in the flesh, but in the spirit, if so be that the spirit of God dwell in you. Now if any man have not the Spirit of Christ, he is none of his.

10 And if Christ be in you, the body is dead because of sin; but the spirit is life because of righteousness.

11 But if the spirit of him that raised up Jesus from the dead dwell in you, he that raised up Christ from the dead shall quicken your mortal bodies by his spirit that dwelleth in you.

12 Therefore, brethren, we are debtors, not to the flesh, to live after the flesh.

13 *For if ye live after the flesh, ye shall die: but if ye through the spirit do mortify the deeds of the body, ye shall live.*

NEW TESTAMENT (1 CORINTHIANS 12:1-11)

1   Now concerning spiritual *gift,* brethren, I would not have you ignorant.

2   Ye know that ye were Gentiles, carried away unto these dumb idols, even as ye were led.

3   Wherefore I give you to understand, that no man speaking by the spirit of God calleth Jesus accursed: and *that* no man can say that Jesus is the Lord, but by the Holy Ghost.

4   Now there are diversities of gifts, but the same spirit.

5   And there are differences of administrations, but the same Lord.

6   And there are diversities of operations, but it is the same God which worketh all in all.

7   ***But the manifestation of the spirit is given to every man to profit withal.***

8   For to one is given by the spirit the word of wisdom; to another the word of knowledge by the same spirit;

9 To another faith by the same spirit; to another the gifts of healing by the same spirit;

10 To another the working of miracles; to another prophecy; to another discerning of spirits; to another *divers* kinds of tongues; to another the interpretation of tongues:

11 ***But all these worketh that one and the self-same Spirit, dividing to every man severally as he will.***

Once you enter into the light, you will be able to recognize the selfish acts of the Ego and start to change your way of thinking. After all, your world view is created by your individual thought patterns.

Don't think that this monster will just disappear overnight. Consider this; the Ego is comparable to a person that is addicted to drugs. Surely a person can get into a drug treatment program; but the journey to becoming drug free is actually the challenge. Remember: the Ego feeds on itself and if its life support system begins to dwindle, it becomes desperate and will try anything to recapture what it has lost. You have to stand fast and recognize the Ego for what it is and reject its attempts to regain control over your thinking.

You must stay awake to the divine spirit within yourself and you will be guided to destroy this monster that resides in you. If you do this and have faith in your true self, there will be no fear.

For just like light and darkness, faith and fear cannot occupy the same space.

PART FOUR

DESTROYING THIS MONSTER

THE SPITITUAL DEFINITION OF "SELF"

Self- The spiritual definition of self is the ***total being*** of one wrapped up in a universe of "oneness." Focusing on certain spiritual elements of "Self" can destroy this monster that feeds on itself. By tapping into your true divine self you will be able to bring light to this darkness in which the Ego operates. ***As we all know, when light comes darkness must flee.*** The following are some of these elements:

Self-**assertion**-Self assertion is defined as the act of asserting one's own rights and wishes, or views. In the spirit realm, you will know that all is yours for the asking. You will maintain your connection with the spirit or true self. ***The Ego must flee.***

Self*-assured**-Self assured is defined as having or showing confidence in oneself. Once you tap into your true divine self, you will be confident that anything is possible and that there is no box. Through your true divine self, you will acquire self assurance and your life will be marvelously changed. You will realize that you possess within you a divine power that cannot be challenged by outside forces. ***The Ego must flee.

Self*-composed**-To possess or display control over one's emotions. Denying the Ego the opportunity to control your emotions will lead to higher conscious decisions and a more rewarding life. ***The Ego must flee.

Self*-confessed**-To confess by one's own admissions. To confess that the spirit of Christ is in you and step back to allow it to lead you through life is something that the Ego despises. You will find that ***fear will be replaced by faith. They cannot occupy the same space. ***The Ego must flee.***

Self-**confidence**-Having self-confidence is to show confidence in oneself or one's abilities. In the spirit realm of self, there is no question as to what you are capable of doing. You will be very confident in all things you endeavor to do. ***The Ego must flee.***

Self-**controlled**-To possess or display control of one's desires or actions. Tapping into the true divine self will allow you to discover your true purpose so that you have complete control over your life. You will deny insatiable appetites of the flesh. ***The Ego must flee.***

Self-**defense**-Defense against attack on oneself... The Ego will put up a fight to maintain control of your life. But once you connect with the true self located in the spirit realm, the Ego will be massacred. ***The Ego must flee.***

Self-**destruct**-To destroy oneself or itself. In order to become acquainted with your true divine self, you must create thought patterns that will cause the Ego to destroy itself. Once you realize the power of the true self in the spirit realm, you will begin to exhibit characteristics that will ultimately cause the Ego to self-destruct…a form of denying yourself. ***The Ego must flee.***

Self*-determination**-The freedom to decide matters for oneself…You will find that you are in complete control of your decisions and not operating at the whim of the Ego disguising itself as you. ***The Ego must flee.

Self*-discipline**-To train and control oneself for personal improvement…Once you meet your true divine self, you will find that you will be driven to seek understanding that will improve your journey to fulfilling the purpose for which you are here. ***The Ego must flee.

Self*-educated**-To be educated by oneself. You will find that the spirit realm of the true self will provide you with more education than you can get in any institution. Once you tap into the true divine self, you will be shown many things the average man cannot see because most people are grounded in the darkness of the Ego. ***The Ego must flee.

Self*-effacing**-Not draw attention to oneself; modest. You will experience a level of peace inside that does not need confirmation from outside. ***The Ego must flee.

Self*-esteem**-Satisfaction with oneself… You will realize that you are created in the likeness of God and gifted with the power of God within you. You will not seek the elements of life in the external, for they do not exist. ***The Ego must flee.

Self*-evident**-Requiring no proof or explanation… You will know that you are spiritually connected. Nor will you desire or seek confirmation from any outside source, including religious institutions. ***The Ego must flee.

Self*-examination**-To inspect and analyze in detail…You will constantly check yourself for staying awake to the true divine self. ***The Ego must flee.

Self*-expression**-The expression of one's own personality as through speech or art… once you tap into your true divine self, you will find that there is no limit to your creativity. There is no box. ***The Ego must flee.

***Self*-fulfilling**-Achieving fulfillment as a result of having been expected or predicted…The true divine self will create an expectancy of great things to come that will bring you inner bliss and joy. *The Ego must flee.*

***Self*-help**-The act or example of providing for self rather than relying on help from others… You will realize that everything you need is within you for the asking. *The Ego must flee.*

Self-image-One's conception of self…you will be able to recognize the true divine self and realize how beautiful you really are. You will no longer have to wear masks. *The Ego must flee.*

Self-knowledge-Knowledge of one's own nature, abilities, and limitations…you will realize the limitations of the flesh and the unlimited power of the spirit. *The Ego must flee.*

Self-less-Without concern for oneself; unselfish… you will no longer be selfish and your world view will become that of oneness within the universe. *The Ego must flee.*

Self-**possession**-Full command of one's feelings and behavior; presence of mind...you will allow the divine self within you to guide your every move in life. ***The ego must flee.***

Self-**preservation**-The instinct to preserve oneself from harm or destruction... You will be able to instantly recognize carnal generated thoughts and shut them down before they cause you any harm. ***The Ego must flee.***

Self-**realization**-The fulfillment by oneself of one's potential...you will be able to tap into your true purpose which will provide you with everything you need to reach your full potential. ***The Ego must flee.***

Self-**regulating**-Regulating oneself without outside control...it will not matter what others have to say. You will be guided by your true divine self to regulate your every move. You will be in total control of your life. ***The Ego must flee.***

Self-**reliance**-Reliance on one's own resources... you will find that your internal cup of resources will not only fill up but it will run over. ***The Ego must flee.***

***Self*-respect**-Proper respect for oneself…You will walk after your true self which will automatically create an enormous amount of respect, even if misunderstood. *The Ego must flee*.

***Self*-restraint**-Restrain imposed on one's emotions, desires, or conduct; self controlled… You will realize that if the true divine self is guiding you, it will lift you to a higher level of understanding which will yield total self control. *The Ego must flee*.

Self-sacrifice-Amazingly, this is one of the major factors for allowing your true divine self to lead you; however, there is no definition found for this in the dictionary. Did God give his only begotten son for us? What are you willing to sacrifice? *The Ego must flee*.

PART FIVE

CONCLUSION

"The world is encountering a spiritual deficit that reflects our need to consciously get on the path of our sacred quest. The solution to individual and global problems is to overcome the spiritual deficit. When you make the shift in consciousness allowing yourself to be an agent of heightened awareness, you are contributing to the transformation of our world."

—Dr. Wayne W. Dyer

We are in the information age and, if you have a computer, there is an icon that reads "**Recycle Bin**." To get your computer to move faster and reserve space for new information you have to move old files to the recycle bin. Now the recycle bin will allow you to recover these files at will for re-use; unless you hit delete and the files are gone forever.

Points to remember:

A.	One of the first things you have to do to destroy this monster that feeds on itself is to create not a recycle bin but a ***"trash bin"*** and move your past to this bin. ***You have to recognize that you are a product of your past which has really not been you.*** You have been dancing to the tunes of external forces that were sketched into your mind by the Ego. All of these sketches have resulted in a state of "***closed mindedness***." Nothing can get in and nothing can come out. ***Take all these selfish traits that the Ego feeds on and dump them into the trash bin and then hit "delete."*** Get rid of these selfish traits forever. ***Do not allow an option for recovery.***

B.	The *Course in Miracles* puts it this way: "*To be born again is to let the past go, and look without condemnation upon the present... You are but asked to let the future go, and place it in God's hands. And you will see by your experience that you have laid the past and the present in His hands as well, because the past will punish you no more and future dread will now be meaningless".*

C.   Your personal history has been guided by an erroneous character known as the carnal mind or Ego. The Ego has worked hard planting seeds to convince you that you are an individual that requires many masks to function in your daily living. Ultimately, you have yielded to the fruits of this planting and have loaded up your trunk with masks. In the process of deleting your personal history, you need to remove all these masks and start anew.

D.   You have been "***hood winked***"…who you are is not in your name, it is not in your physical body, it is not in your occupation, it is not in your relationships, it is not in your race or religion, it is not in what others say you are…all of these things are tools used by the Ego to set us apart from each other. Instead you are united with all souls in a universe of oneness no matter what your Ego-induced packaging says you are.

E.   When you begin to tap into your true divine self, you will develop a more loving nature. This frightens the Ego and it will do everything it can to prevent this kind of approach. The Ego thrives on self concepts that produce conflict and strife. It will call out all its troops (those being led by the Ego) and access an arsenal of falseness and illusions to initiate a full scale assault to block your movement to a higher awareness of your true divine self.

F.   Dr. Wayne Dyer puts it like this: *As you continue to consult your higher self, you will affect the collective consciousness and force those who are hanging onto the ego-based system to relax their hold, and then the collective ego dries up and withers away.*

G.   Nisargadatta Maharaj states it like this: *"That which sees all this, and nothing too, is the inner teacher. He alone is, all else only appears to be. He is your own self, your hope and assurance of freedom; find him and cling to him and you will be saved and safe".*

Man has searched and will continue to search for answers as to who we are, where we came from, why are we here, where are we going and to whom do we answer. It is so difficult for man because he is asking the wrong source…the Ego. The Ego knows no truth and it cannot provide any real answers. It will provide you with misleading sources and sell you illusions that appear to be so real that if you are not awake to the true divine self, you will be led into an action which I term "*looping*." Never finding any truth, only going around and around in circles…never reaching your destination.

Yet the answer is so simple…all the answers to all your questions are found within the true divine self. Once you discover your true divine self and destroy this monster called carnality or the Ego, you will be on a journey to heavenly things… good things…right now!

PEACE!